THE ISLAND NATION

Christine Bacon

THE ISLAND NATION

OBERON BOOKS
LONDON

WWW.OBERONBOOKS.COM

First published in 2016 by Oberon Books Ltd
521 Caledonian Road, London N7 9RH
Tel: +44 (0) 20 7607 3637 / Fax: +44 (0) 20 7607 3629
e-mail: info@oberonbooks.com
www.oberonbooks.com

A catalogue record for this book is available from the British
Library.

PB ISBN: 9781786820662
E ISBN: 9781786820679

Cover photo by Kumar Nav
Marketing image by Sian Jones

Visit www.oberonbooks.com to read more about all our books
and to buy them. You will also find features, author interviews and
news of any author events, and you can sign up for e-newsletters
so that you're always first to hear about our new releases.

Characters

NILA
Tamil woman in northern Sri Lanka, early 20s

ERIK
Norwegian peace mediator, mid 40s

REBECCA
British UN aid worker, 30s

BALASINGHAM
Tamil Tiger negotiator, 60s

KP
Tamil Tiger arms dealer, 50s

CHANDRIKA
President of Sri Lanka, 40+

JENNY
Rebecca's boss, American, 40+

SANATH
Official from the Sri Lankan Foreign Ministry, mid 30s

NICK
British aid worker, 30s

Doubling:

BALASINGHAM/KP

CHANDRIKA/JENNY

NICK/SANATH

All other parts played by the cast.

The play is written for six actors.

NILA is at home in the Vanni, northern Sri Lanka. It is late 2004. She is 21. She is listening to some Tamil/Hindu music on an old, bad quality Walkman as she walks through her village. She walks past cadjan huts, concrete houses, Tiger propaganda on walls, pictures of Prabhakaran, the Tiger cemetery, palmyra trees and then a narrow crack between concrete walls where the sea is visible. Gradually, the crack between the walls becomes bigger and NILA is standing and facing the sea while practising her dance moves to the music she is listening to.

ERIK waits to board a plane at an airport (1999).

BALASINGHAM is wearily getting ready in a London flat in 1999. He puts on his shirt, tie and suit jacket. He then switches on a light in the shape of Sri Lanka with Tamil Eelam (the territory controlled by the Tamil Tigers at the time) illuminated in neon. He presses another switch and the frame around a portrait of the Tamil Tiger leader Vellupilai Prabakharan lights up. He pulls out a small, fading Tamil Tiger flag on a stand from a drawer in the table and places it on a table in an Indian restaurant.

REBECCA is at an airport. She has a CD walkman and she plays an audio guide and looks through a guide book about Sri Lanka she has bought at the airport. She has a duty free bag with several Twix bars inside. Hackneyed traditional music plays under cheesy voiceover.

VOICEOVER: Sri Lanka, formerly Ceylon, is an island nation which hangs like a pearl earring off the south coast of India. The population of 21 million is ethnically and linguistically diverse. Sinhalese Buddhists are the majority, but you'll also find Tamils, Muslims and Christians there. After almost four centuries of colonisation, first by the Portuguese, followed by the Dutch and then the British, Sri Lanka gained its independence in 1948. An island paradise, where you can discover world heritage sites, travel back in time to an era of kings and temples, explore mountains and waterfalls, enjoy the wildlife, and of course, relax at the end of the day on one of those glorious beaches.

ERIK enters BALASINGHAM's space wearing an ill-fitting suit and carries a rucksack on his back. He and BALASINGHAM shake hands. The subsequent scenes between them play out over six years.

VOICE OVER: The leader of the Tamil Tigers is Vellupillai Prabhakaran, a charismatic figure who demands absolute loyalty and sacrifice and has led the movement since the armed resistance began in 1983. The Tigers hold a significant amount of territory in the north of the island. Their stated aim is to establish their own separate state called Tamil Eelam. Sri Lanka is also renowned for its tea …

ERIK: Mr. Balasingham

BALASINGHAM: Please sit

ERIK sits.

I appreciate you coming so early.

ERIK: That's not a problem.

BALASINGHAM: My wife forbids me from working after lunch now that I'm so long in the tooth.

ERIK: I understand.

BALASINGHAM: Your flight was OK?

ERIK: Fine.

BALASINGHAM: And the traffic from Heathrow?

ERIK: I travelled by tube.

BALASINGHAM: We don't know each other Mr Solheim. And this is a matter of … we need to ease ourselves in. Don't you agree?

A WAITER appears and puts a teapot and teacup in front of BALASINGHAM.

ERIK: Not for me thank you.

BALASINGHAM: I'm afraid these sorts of procedures don't function very well without tea and biscuits. Rule number one. They must have taught you that, surely?

ERIK nods to WAITER who places a teacup in front of ERIK and he pours himself some tea. WAITER places a plate of biscuits on the table. ERIK takes one.

ERIK: Thank you.

BALASINGHAM: People from all over the world have been drawn to our struggle. Most of them have been a flash in the pan. Some have betrayed our trust. What is it that has piqued your interest?

ERIK: I travelled to Sri Lanka last year to stay with a good friend. He offered me to sit in his house and … no journalists with cameras, no children would be around, so I would have all that time to concentrate on writing my autobiography.

BALASINGHAM: What a curious thing. You can't be more than …

ERIK: I had resigned as leader of my party and … well, if I wrote about it ten years after the event –

BALASINGHAM: Ah, I see. Please, go on.

ERIK: I was not particularly interested in Sri Lankan affairs. Or, I should say, I was as interested in Sri Lankan affairs as much as I was interested in Ecuadorian affairs, or Burundian affairs … in that it's a fascinating part of the world. And well, you know the rest of the story.

BALASINGHAM: You Norwegians have a special gift for affiliating yourselves with notorious rebel groups.

We see CHANDRIKA at a table in the back of the restaurant. The lamp on her table is in the shape of Sri Lanka with the entire border lit up.

CHANDRIKA: Mr Solheim.

ERIK: Madam President.

CHANDRIKA: I am giving you permission to initiate secret discussions with their 'Chief Negotiator' Mr. Balasingham and let's see where it goes. This is something I wish to announce only when the time is right.

ERIK: Of course.

BALASINGHAM: And so we are permitted to begin the talks about talks.

CHANDRIKA: *(To ERIK.)* I'm intrigued. How will you sell this murderous faraway conflict with a terrorist group to the mild-mannered Norwegians?

ERIK: The official line? We are a nation that considers world peace to be in our deepest interest.

BALASINGHAM and CHANDRIKA laugh. ERIK laughs along.

These kinds of initiatives are actually very popular domestically. Of course it's also an excellent way for a tiny nation to get attention from the rest of the world. Otherwise, why would the major powers spend one second on us?

BALASINGHAM: That's better. Rule number 2:

WAITER fills BALASINGHAM's and ERIK's glasses with white wine.

Move onto stronger substances once things have warmed up a bit.

CHANDRIKA: And *you* are an ambitious politician. What a shame for an ambitious politician to be to be born in a country a stable and as agreeable as Norway. This will give you something to sink your teeth into. I want regular reports.

BALASINGHAM: *(To ERIK.)* We won't get anywhere with her. She tells the world she is some sort of goddess of peace. Sending 50,000 troops into Jaffna to wipe us out is a 'war for peace'.

CHANDRIKA suddenly recoils. She puts her hand over her right eye. WAITER goes to her aid and applies a bandage made of a Sri Lankan flag to her eye. She addresses the nation.

CHANDRIKA: The Tamil Tigers have attempted to snatch my life. They have robbed me of an eye. Seared me with the weapons of hatred and terror. Look at my wounds.

BALASINGHAM: Oh, here we go with the theatrics … the Buddhist pilgrim speaks.

ERIK: *(To BALASINGHAM.)* This is absolutely counter-productive.

BALASINGHAM: Yes, but Prabhakaran will say the government has killed many in our ranks …

ERIK: There is a huge difference of perception in killing a guerrilla fighter in north eastern Sri Lanka and the suicide bomb attack of an elected head of state.

CHANDRIKA: This problem is now the only one left for my government. For the sake of my country and my people, who I love very much, we have to negotiate with Mr Prabakharan *if* he is willing to give up his devilish ways. I have given Norway a formal mandate to facilitate these talks.

BALASINGHAM: *(Laughs – to ERIK.)* Congratulations! Sounds like you got the job!

ERIK: *(Surprised – to CHANDRIKA.)* Some warning would have been useful.

WAITER re-fills the wine glasses.

ERIK: Other nations are only going to isolate you after this.

BALASINGHAM: This is Prabhakaran's movement. I am the only member who is older than him, and as I am not a military man, I'm not a threat to him. My asset is that I know a lot that he does not about the outside world … and sometimes he listens.

ERIK: He has agreed to open these peace negotiations. He has agreed to meet with me. That is something we can build on.

BALASINGHAM starts to wipe his brow intermittently with his napkin.

OK: Pre-conditions for a ceasefire …

BALASINGHAM: I will discuss everything in due course, but you need to know what the Sri Lankan government has done to the Tamil people before we can begin.

ERIK: I've been well briefed about that.

BALASINGHAM: This is my fourth attempt at peace talks. This is only your first.

ERIK eats a poppadom and calls the WAITER over and asks for more wine as BALASINGHAM continues. CHANDRIKA listens in.

It is in the nature of the Tamil people to make sure their children spend most of their time studying. They are very focused on that. After the British left Sri Lanka, the Sinhalese majority, felt there were too many Tamils getting into university, and into top jobs. So, the man running for President at the time said vote me in and I'll replace English as the official language of the country with Sinhala – a language we Tamils do not understand. And he won. It didn't take long for the intended effect to be achieved – the civil service was almost entirely Sinhalese. Who was that man? *Her* father!

CHANDRIKA: One of his few mistakes.

BALASINGHAM: Anti-Tamil massacres in 1956, 1958, 1961. Then they started demanding higher marks from Tamil students for university admission than Sinhalese. More massacres in…

CHANDRIKA and BALASINGHAM: 1974, 1977,

CHANDRIKA, BALASINGHAM and ERIK: 1979, 1981 and

ERIK: July 1983.

BALASINGHAM: Black July.

CHANDRIKA: Yes, the Tamil minority have been treated unfairly. I don't disagree.

BALASINGHAM: Thousands of Tamils singled out and hacked to death, burnt alive in the course of a few days. Huge numbers moved from the south to the north or chose exile abroad. And thousands more decided to join the armed struggle.

CHANDRIKA: *(To ERIK.)* All Sri Lankans know about brutality. Not just Tamils. My father, the former President – assassinated when I was 14 by a Buddhist monk. My husband was riddled with bullets outside our home in front of myself and our 2 young children during a Marxist insurgency in the south. In broad daylight. Everybody in Sri Lanka has a story about brutality.

While BALASINGHAM is speaking, he takes medication washed down with wine. He dabs at his forehead with a Tiger flag and showing signs of gradually increasing pain/discomfort/fatigue for the rest of the scene.

BALASINGHAM: We tried 30 years of non-violent resistance and there was no progress. We fight for a separate state, or we shall remain sitting under the table of the Sinhalese and picking up the crumbs.

CHANDRIKA walks over to the table and stands over it, picking at some of the food as she speaks.

CHANDRIKA: That sort of poetic rubbish might work on the peasants they control through the barrel of a gun! And the diaspora whose money is extorted to pay for the war machine. *(To ERIK.)* Guerrilla fighters parading around with those cyanide capsules about their necks. Do you think they could run a nation?

BALASINGHAM: Ha! Her government is in in total disarray!

CHANDRIKA: This group who cares so *deeply* for Tamil people, systematically murdered the moderate Tamil leaders who were in favour of non-violent reform.

ERIK: None of this is within the scope of the talks …

CHANDRIKA: These 'freedom fighters' who are always going on about minority rights, forced more than 70,000 Tamil-speaking Muslims from their homes. That's what they do with *their* minorities.

BALASINGHAM: Extrajudicial killings. Disappearances. Branding. Rape. Slamming testicles in desk drawers/

CHANDRIKA: /Oh, and the angelic Tigers have of course never used torture?

ERIK: We are not here to discuss the shortcomings of each party.

CHANDRIKA: Child soldiers. Suicide bombings. Calculated attacks on civilians in the south.

BALASINGHAM: We have a military operation, organisational command and capacity, a police force, TV station, courts, a naval and air unit – the first time in history a non-state actor created a private air force. And we control 15% of the vote. We are not a rag-tag bunch of guerrillas in the jungle.

CHANDRIKA: It's true. That's true. They have given us a run for our money.

ERIK: A lot of this work can be done much more productively if the guns are silent. I have drafted the basis of an agreement.

He hands the paperwork to CHANDRIKA and BALASINGHAM.

CHANDRIKA: *(To ERIK while looking over the draft agreement.)* We cannot give the impression that the Prabhakaran can have access to you whenever he wants to. Contact should be a reward for good behaviour.

ERIK: I think that is a mistake. It has been very useful meeting Balasingham on a regular basis but very few non-Tamils talk to Prabhakaran and the more high level visits, the more discussion we can engage him in, 24 hours a day if necessary, the better the outcome will be. On the few times you have allowed me to go to the north of Sri Lanka to speak with him and he tells me he will stop the killing, it stops *the next day.*

CHANDRIKA: *(To ERIK.)* You understand how important the visual impression is in politics. That murderous scum must not be taken as seriously on the international stage as the sovereign government of Sri Lanka. He killed the former Prime Minister of India. He almost killed me. No ceasefire yet, I want to see some progress first. That man will not act in good faith.

WAITER passes CHANDRIKA a note. She reads it and sits. She is shaken.

CHANDRIKA: *(To the press.)* I have ordered an immediate investigation to determine how and why a 14-man Tamil Tiger suicide squad was able to infiltrate the security of our national airport and once again cause deep and lasting pain to our nation. We need to brace ourselves for the economic repercussions of such an attack.

(To ERIK.) Why do people blow themselves into pieces for that man?

WAITER passes ERIK a piece of paper.

ERIK: *(To BALASINGHAM.)* There's a new player. Madam President has a power-sharing arrangement with a new Prime Minister. And he is ready for a ceasefire agreement.

BALANSINGHAM: We circumvent the President?

ERIK: The Prime Minister has the authority to sign.

BALASINGHAM: They are from opposing parties. Their dislike for each other is well known.

ERIK: This is a window and it will not be open for long. Look through that window. You must make Prabhakaran sign.

BALASINGHAM produces an envelope. ERIK smiles and takes the envelope. Spotlight appears on ERIK as he addresses the international press.

ERIK: On this historic day, 22 February 2002, The Norwegian government is very pleased to announce that the Sri Lankan government and Tamil Tiger leaders formally agreed to an internationally monitored ceasefire yesterday, opening the way to full-scale peace talks.

ERIK: We need to agree dates and venues for the talks. Thailand will host the first round.

BALASINGHAM: What will we do about the flags?

ERIK: Flags?

BALASINGHAM: At the talks. On the tables. The little flags on little stands.

ERIK: Ah… A Tiger flag in the room will be seen as the government accepting that flag and therefore your claim of a separate state. There will be no progress in these talks until the separate state issue is dealt with.

WAITER whispers into BALASINGHAM'S ear.

BALASINGHAM: Prabhakaran is willing to put it in writing that a federal arrangement with power sharing and no separate state could be *explored* in these talks.

This is an electric moment for ERIK. The WAITER approaches ERIK and hands him a note.

WAITER: A message from UN Secretary General Kofi Annan

ERIK reads it.

ERIK: 'Congratulations on Sri Lanka'.

CHANDRIKA: *(To ERIK.)* They've done almost nothing they said they would do. Hundreds of ceasefire violations.

ERIK: *(To CHANDRIKA.)* Madam President – the ceasefire has held for over 2 years. The economy is improving. Aid is flowing in. Tourists are coming back. Very few deaths have occurred in this time. What you wanted was to expose the Tigers to a world beyond the war zone and make them more open to compromise and this has worked.
The negotiating teams who were very stiff with each other at the first round of talks are now having jacuzzis together at the end of the day.

CHANDRIKA: While you and the negotiating teams sit in jacuzzis in cities around the world chatting about promises and modalities, Prabakharan and his men are building up their military capabilities.

BALASINGHAM: She's doing the same thing.

CHANDRIKA: I'm in control here. Not them, not you and certainly not our Prime Minister.

WAITER starts to clear the table.

ERIK: *(To BALASINGHAM.)* We're stepping back for a while. She and the Prime Minister need to sort out their problems before we can establish who we are actually negotiating with.

ERIK: *(To the press.)* The peace process is at its lowest ebb.

Visual/audio of waves/tsunami.

2.

REBECCA's phone (circa 2004) rings. She answers it.

REBECCA: Hello

NICK: Rebecca?

REBECCA: Who's calling?

NICK: Nick. From uni.

REBECCA: Oh! Nick. Are you not in …

NICK: Yeah.

REBECCA: Fucking hell.

NICK: Yeah, yeah.

REBECCA: Shit.

NICK: I'm calling anyone I can think of. We're … we just don't know how to deal with what's going on. And I thought if you were in India – are you …?

REBECCA: Yeah. Mumbai. Yeah.

NICK: I thought you could get over here quickly and … I'm sort of going crazy.

REBECCA: Right yeah. Sorry, you've just –

NICK: It's coming out of the blue and all that, but … we just need people and I could do with someone, I mean I'm basically on my own up here running on adrenaline and fags.

REBECCA: For a couple of weeks or so – is that what you mean?

NICK: Just get a ticket to Colombo.

REBECCA: And then I –

NICK: 16,000 dead up here. Swallowed by the sea and spat out. In 20 minutes. I'm in Tamil Tiger territory. In the north. I can sort you out once you're in country.

REBECCA: Can I bring anything up for you?

NICK: Twix bars. Anything with chocolate in. More fags. DVDs about anything. And booze.

3.

BALASINGHAM and CHANDRIKA look directly at each other. ERIK and the WAITER seize their chance and start setting the table again. They put out fancy napkins, a rose in a vase, polish the glasses. CHANDRIKA and BALASINGHAM walk towards the table and tentatively pull out a chair.

ANNOUNCEMENT: In the aftermath of the 2004 Boxing Day tsunami, Sri Lankans of all stripes are calling for peace. Television debates and newspaper articles are full of impassioned pleas to put past differences aside and turn the fragile ceasefire into a meaningful peace process. A golden opportunity.

BALASINGHAM sits. CHANDRIKA almost takes her seat but then chooses to walk away. WAITER brings the bill to the table and gives it to ERIK.

WAITER: The bill sir.

Visual of the white robe and maroon scarf of President Mahinda Rajapakse.

ANNOUNCEMENT: Mahinda Rajapakse assumes the office of President of Sri Lanka in the November 2005 elections after a campaign fought with a hard line stance on the Tamil Tiger issue. A 45% increase in military expenditure has been approved by Parliament.

4.

NICK and REBECCA remove their boots and surgical masks and gloves and start cleaning their nostrils with soap.

NICK: Beer o'clock?

REBECCA nods and takes one.

NICK: We're getting there.

REBECCA: It just never goes away does it?

NICK: Have you been putting the menthol stuff on?

REBECCA nods.

REBECCA: No vomiting today though.

NICK: Yeah.

REBECCA: *(Looks at a box.)* What's left?

NICK: We haven't started on the *Sex in the City* box set yet.

REBECCA: What season?

NICK: Four. Aidan's back! She should never have broken up with him.

REBECCA: I feel like I should have cried more than I have.

NICK: You didn't lose anyone. I suppose.

REBECCA: But when you see what we see. And the kids.

NICK: You just switch, don't you, into clinical mode.

REBECCA: Because I've never really seen death before this. Except for my granny in a casket, with make up on and her hair all brushed nicely.

NICK: Check you out! The hardened humanitarian.

REBECCA: Have you heard them talking about … all that superstitious stuff.

NICK: About the Americans planting a nuclear bomb in the ocean?

REBECCA: Like they're being punished because the world thinks they are terrorists.

NICK: There's loads of money sloshing around. You could start up a public education thing.

REBECCA: Like a presentation? About how tsunamis happen and how it's affected other places.

NICK: There's a cricket project, a counselling project, a bloody flower-growing project for all we know. Go talk to my boss about it.

REBECCA: You could take it around the villages. Get some interpreters. Hang a sheet up. Get a projector.

NICK: Talk to him. I'll go with you if you like.

Pulls out some sleeping tablets.

Want a couple?

REBECCA takes 2 and swallows them with her beer.

No rush to get back to India then?

REBECCA: Ah, I was a bit of a lost soul there. I kept going from one charity to the next doing bits and bobs.

NICK hums the Sex and the City theme tune.

Go on then.

NICK: We've always got Manhattan darling.

5.

BALASINGHAM has removed his tie and suit jacket.

BALASINGHAM: I've begged Prabhakaran not to return to war. You've helped us to achieve what no one else managed. A ceasefire that saved many lives. You got some business in Sudan from this, no? I heard that Nepal has been courting you as well. Now you can write your second autobiography.

ERIK: Why can't he see what you see?

BALASINGHAM: We are sitting in London – formerly the epicentre of the world, with all of the wealth and weaponry they could possibly acquire, and they learned the lesson of ignoring and supressing nationalist aspirations. They finally had to say to Ireland, one of the smallest, most impoverished nations in the world – OK – we will give you 26 of the 32 counties.

ERIK picks up his papers and his rucksack.

ERIK: Everyone else is subordinate to him.

BALASINGHAM: You have to keep trying.

ERIK and BALASINGHAM shake hands.

BALASINGHAM: It's a rare cancer. A small personal tragedy.

ERIK: Goodbye Bala.

ERIK stands behind a podium at BALASINGHAM's funeral.

ERIK: For a long period of time I came to London every week to speak with Bala. He was a brilliant person, he was the overshadowing influence of the peace process, an intellectual and a very decent man. He had a profound understanding of how the rest of the world is working which is of great importance. In this process, he was one of the very, very few people who never lied to me.

I've not come to this funeral to make a political speech, but Bala was a political person. I think it's very sad that his passing away is in a period when he will have been most needed. The spirit of Bala would be to pick up the mantle and try to find a way to ensure there are no more unnecessary deaths in Sri Lanka. Thank you Bala for the friendship you have shown.

6.

REBECCA and NILA are looking at a power point presentation.

REBECCA: Have you given many presentations before?

NILA: In school and some times at university.

REBECCA: Do you get nervous?

NILA: A little bit. But when I begin, it's OK.

REBECCA: What do you think of it?

NILA: It's good.

REBECCA: Do you think it will be clear?

NILA: It's good to explain the reality.

REBECCA: But … ?

NILA: It's good.

REBECCA Refers to a map of the area.

REBECCA: We'll start in PTK tomorrow.

NILA: Puthukkudiyiruppu

REBECCA: Yeah that

NILA: Puthuk-kudiy-iruppu

REBECCA: Poothook kewdy

NILA: Kudiy

REBECCA: Koo-dee

NILA: Irippu. Puthukkudiyiruppu. It's not so difficult. Just like all the other internationals.

REBECCA: Yeah, sorry. Do you want to do a run-through in Tamil then? Rehearsal?

NILA is hesitant.

NILA: I wanted to tell you that I think when the presentation is over, people will have a lot of emotion. And we are presenting in many schools. The children have lost parents so they will be remembering.

REBECCA: Oh. It's just, we can't change the presentation. I've spent the last few months finalising this with the Geological Survey. They've signed off on it now.

NILA: My mother was killed by the wave.

REBECCA: Oh. I'm. I'll find something else for you to do. Behind the scenes maybe.

NILA: No, no. I can do it no problem. But I think –

REBECCA: We could do it in a different way?

NILA: Yes. With something happier at the end.

REBECCA rummages through the DVD box and pulls out a Tom and Jerry DVD.

REBECCA: Everyone loves *Tom and Jerry*.

7.

REBECCA and JENNY at a bar in Colombo sitting near each other.

JENNY: Tourist?

REBECCA: No. No. I'm with an NGO in the Vanni. *(Points up.)*

JENNY: Tsunami reconstruction?

REBECCA: I'm running a public education thing around what causes tsunamis and/

JENNY: /Oh – you're that Tom and Jerry woman, right? Someone from UNICEF was telling us about you.

REBECCA: They think I'm mad.

JENNY: Joseph is a prick. I thought it sounded fun.

REBECCA: You go from talking about tectonic plates and doom and gloom … I had 500 people on a beach in Mullativu who had lost up to 28 members of their family crying with laughter for half an hour. That's good therapy in my book.

JENNY: Did you have to get it cleared with the Tigers?

REBECCA: That was part of the reason I chose Tom and Jerry. Because you can't play anything that could be interpreted as … that they would see as delivering the wrong message. But what could they say about a cat chasing a mouse?

JENNY: You know a few of them do you?

REBECCA: They're the only game in town up there so yeah we've had quite a bit to do with them.

JENNY: A lot of my colleagues hate dealing with them.

REBECCA: They rule the place with an iron fist, it has to be said, but individually, really nice people. My mum and dad came up to visit a few weeks back and when we were going through the checkpoint, they were all like oh, would you like some tea and cake and all of this stuff and my dad sort of whispers to me – you know, these are the loveliest terrorists I've ever met. Collectively though, yeah, they're ruthless. But I get along with a lot of them. Mutual respect sort of thing.

JENNY: Do they really think they're going to get their own state up there?

REBECCA: Yeah. They believe it. They've had a rough deal – and they don't want to live like slaves under the Sri Lankan government. What do I say to that?

JENNY: We can all see what's coming. You must see it too. The ceasefire is technically still in place, but I mean – the number of checkpoints everywhere. And look at that soldier – stroking his Kalashnikov like it's his cock or something. This 'peace' is evaporating in front of our eyes.

REBECCA: You do feel it, under the skin of the place.

JENNY: What are you running away from?

REBECCA: Uh … dunno.

JENNY: Everyone in this game is. I cheated, he cheated. Marriage ended. Lost the house.

REBECCA: Maybe it's small town syndrome. Drugs maybe? I did quite a lot of drugs at one point.

JENNY: Finding yourself. That's standard. People assume being a humanitarian is a selfless kind of thing don't they?

REBECCA: Yeah.

JENNY: But the ego stuff is huge. I used to work till I couldn't stay awake anymore and I loved that elevated state. I was one of those who got on the next flight out when some new disaster hit. You must be in that kind of honeymoon phase?

REBECCA: I'm having fun. It's exciting. Politically, it's really interesting, watching this whole thing unfold, having an insight into that. Having dinner under the stars, under a mango tree with some pretty hard core people who have shot down helicopters and done all kinds of crazy shit and are quite happy to show me pictures and tell me stories. Well it beats sitting in a pub on a Tuesday night.

JENNY: Are you interested in working for the UN?

REBECCA: I didn't see that one coming.

JENNY: People are always asking me how to get a job in the UN and I say – honestly, turn up at the next disaster and look busy.

REBECCA: Or go to the right bar and have a beer with the right UN official.

JENNY: That's the other way to do it.

REBECCA: What's the job?

JENNY: We need someone who can liaise with the Tigers on … everything to do with reconstruction. So, there was supposed to be a joint mechanism to make sure foreign aid was distributed evenly

REBECCA: Yeah yeah and the Tigers were pissed off that the money wasn't being sent up north.

JENNY: Exactly – it took six months for that plan to fail miserably … so now, because the government are so paranoid about the Tigers getting their hands on anything that can be used for combat – we have to spend an insane number of man hours getting their OK to take anything across into the north, but then once it's there –

REBECCA: It has to be approved by the Tigers. Locations need to be agreed …

JENNY: You'll get a better salary.

REBECCA: Yep. Yep.

JENNY: Once you're in the UN system, you'll get other postings. You might get a capital city next time.

REBECCA: I only came here on a whim.

JENNY: But you're still here.

REBECCA: I don't know if it's me really. As a career I mean. The kind of things I've heard my colleagues say …

JENNY: It's everyone's favourite rant, me included – nobody is accountable, it' the new colonialism, the big money only goes to the fashionable causes, it takes a year to get consensus on anything and by then you've lost the momentum. And so much of that is true. There are plenty of fucked up things happening. But it's still a way to get basic needs to people who really, really need that stuff. And when you see it on the ground and when someone tells you later that they only survived because an agency brought them water and some food and a tent. Like with anything, anywhere, it's about who goes to that place. Who ends up there. A good water sanitation project in Nigeria could be a disaster in Afghanistan because the individuals sent out to deliver it are assholes.

REBECCA: Can I buy you a drink?

8.

REBECCA and NILA are watching a David Attenborough documentary about the North Pole on REBECCA's laptop. This scene plays out over 2 years.

VOICE OVER: Polar bears travel further than almost any other bears in their search for food. A single polar bear may range 300,000 square kilometres, an area the size of Italy.

NILA: I would love to lie on the ice there.

REBECCA: You wouldn't last very long! You're a good source of meat.

Footage of seals.

NILA: They are so ugly. Just fat with 2 little arms.

REBECCA makes seal noises.

REBECCA: That's the noise they make.

NILA tries. Footage changes. A Hollywood blockbuster (2004).

NILA: Why are you always dressing in these men's clothes?

REEBCCA: It's comfortable.

NILA: Is this what all the women do in the UK?

REBECCA: Lots of them yeah.

NILA: And your hair! You need to use some oil.

REBECCA: Oh, I can't be bothered with all of that.

They are now watching a Bollywood routine.

NILA: She's very beautiful.

REBECCA: This is just so –

NILA: You don't like it?

REBECCA: The singing and dancing about …

NILA: Oh I love it. Do your parents want you to get married soon?

REBECCA: No. They just want me to be OK. As long as I'm happy …

NILA: My mother was not like that.

REBECCA: What was she like then?

NILA: We did not agree about so many things. The last day I saw her we were having argument. I thought about that argument so many times. What I said to her. She only wanted me to have success in my life. Like any mother.

JENNY: Do you have a photo?

NILA takes a picture from the inside of her sari.

NILA: We didn't find her body.

The footage on the screen becomes more distorted, violent. A map shows that the army are advancing and capturing territory.

NILA: What do you tell the UN people when you go to Colombo?

REBECCA: I say it's getting tougher, harder every day. I tell them I'm worried about the civilians here.

NILA: Whatever way we turn, we are in a bad situation.

REBECCA: But if the Tigers just let you leave –

NILA: Without them we have no hope as a people in our own country. I know what they do, but I can't be totally against them. They have stood up to the army and the government for us and if we leave there is no Eelam. This is my home. The Tigers always have a good plan and they always defeat the army. They will never let the Vanni be taken.

9.

ERIK walks towards a microphone.

ERIK: Norway has sent a formal letter to both leaders
requesting responses to five critical questions.
In particular, whether they remain committed to the
ceasefire agreement. This is an unprecedented move,
but we are seriously concerned that the ceasefire is at the
point of breaking down completely.

*Leaflets fall from the sky. NILA picks one up. So does REBECCA.
We hear the dull thuds of shelling a few miles away. A Tamil cadre
speaks over a loudspeaker on an auto-rickshaw.*

10.

VOICE OVER: We are now officially at war. Pack your essential
items and build bunkers. The leaflets the army has
dropped tell you to surrender to them. If you cross into
government territory, the army will torture you or execute
you. Do not leave. We will protect you.

*REBECCA walks into her office in the UN compound reading one of
the leaflets. We hear the 'ping' sound of an incoming email. She reads
it and makes a phone call to JENNY in Colombo. A portrait of Ban
Ki-Moon is hanging in JENNY's office and a UN flag is on her desk.*

JENNY: You got the email.

REBECCA: Phase 5?

JENNY: The government say they cannot guarantee the safety
of UN staff.

REBECCA: When?

JENNY: Within the week.

REBECCA: There must be a way to keep a few of us here …
to at least monitor …

JEENY: I've been back and forth with them. I can't put you in that kind of danger.

REBECCA: If it's too dangerous for us it's too dangerous for everyone. *Their troops* are the biggest threat to our safety – can't we request that they avoid –

JENNY: You need to trust me on this one.

REBECCA: OK. OK. Sorry. This is where I live. And people know us. They trust us.

JENNY: Yeah. We had to evacuate Haiti with a day's notice and we were like beaten dogs boarding the plane. The simple truth of that. My life is worth more than your life.

REBECCA: How am I supposed to look them in the eye?

JENNY: We knew this was coming. They knew it as well. Right now, you need to work with everyone else there and you need to pack up the compound, remove the files and computers, decommission the heavy equipment and leave.

The thuds become louder. We hear an announcement to all in the compound.

VOICE OVER: Birds in the sky. Birds in the sky. Please go immediately to your bunkers until further notice.

JENNY: You need to follow instructions now Rebecca. When you're in Colombo, we'll debrief and try to do what we can.

11.

REBECCA is helping NILA pack her few belongings. She takes a satellite phone out of her rucksack.

REBECCA: You'll need this to re-charge it *(takes out a small solar panel)*. We can text each other. You can have this too *(takes out her iPod and gives it to NILA)*. Here *(takes money out of her pocket and tries to give it to her)*.

NILA: Will you take a photo of me?

REBECCA takes out her camera.

NILA: Wait. *(She adjusts her hair and stands very close to the camera so her face fills the frame.)*

REBECCA takes a couple of photos.

REBECCA: I'll find a way to come back. I'm sorry.

NILA: You should go. It's too dangerous for you here.

Sounds of planes in the sky overhead becomes very loud. REBECCA puts on her flak jacket and a protective helmet and picks up her backpack. As she leaves, she sees NILA standing with her belongings, watching her leave.

12.

REBECCA enters the UN office in Colombo looking dishevelled and enters JENNY's office.

REBECCA: They watched us drive away in an armoured vehicle. Their faces were just blank.

JENNY: We're hopeful it will calm down and we'll get access again – could be a couple of weeks, maybe a month.

REBECCA: There's an army on their doorstep.

JENNY: The government will allow us to take weekly convoys of basic supplies into the war zone, why don't we focus on that for now? Logistically, it'll be … God knows. We'll need your help with making sure the Tigers allow safe passage.

REBECCA: Yeah.

JENNY: But look at you. Right now, I think you should take a few days off. Have a meal. Soak in a tub. Call your parents.

13.

REBECCA is in her hotel room with a towel around her head and is wearing a robe. She's on the phone. NILA lies in a shallow bunker talking to REBECCA.

NILA: Can't sleep.

REBECCA: Me either.

NILA: Is it nice in Colombo?

REBECCA: Not bad.

NILA: What are people saying about us?

REBECCA: The usual. The Tigers must be crushed. How are you managing?

NILA: It's becoming like a routine now. Bunkers day and night sometimes. There's a lady near here who is normally a very posh sort of person and now she is sleeping on the ground like everyone else, and she is complaining that all of her expensive saris are getting damaged. Tell me about your hotel room.

REBECCA: It's got a very nice view. Right on the sea front.

NILA: Is there anyone walking by the sea?

REBECCA: 2 drunk men.

NILA: What else?

REBECCA: A lamp on the bedside table. A TV. A vase with nothing in it. A painting of a monk. I bought some hair oil. It's disgusting! Feels like I dipped my head in ghee.

NILA: You will soon see the difference. All the men will be running after you.

REBECCA: I've washed it three times and it's still all … ugh

NILA: Keep talking.

REBECCA: I can't think of anything.

NILA: Tell me about British recipes.

REBECCA: Bloody hell. I'm not much of a cook … but OK. My regular thing when I was at uni was tuna pasta.

NILA: Oh yes, I have had this one, pasta. It's very chewy.

REBECCA: I suppose it is yeah. So first off, you get yourself an onion, preferably a red one, a tin of tuna, and if you so desire, a tin of sweet corn.

Noise of incoming shelling.

Nila?

NILA: Call me back later.

REBECCA: Yep. Listen to track 42.

NILA hangs up and listens to Track 42 on the iPod.

14.

REBECCA is in Jenny's office.

JENNY: 58 trucks of food, and five 4x4s for the staff.

REBECCA: For 300,000 people? Are the government still peddling their bullshit 70,000 figure? We've got satellites for fuck's sake!

JENNY: It's taken all day for them to concede to this. They aren't even letting the Red Cross bring medicines in now in case the Tigers use them. They want us out within 24 hours. We can use what time we have to survey some of the displaced. But even with assurances, the guys on last week's convoy were terrified one side would bomb them and blame it on the other side.

REBECCA Why don't I go in with the next convoy? A lot of the Tigers know me. It could help?

(REBECCA sends a text message to NILA – I'm coming up next week.)

15.

A large number of people are on the move. Through a loudspeaker we hear a LTTE cadre:

VOICE OVER: We have control of the frontline and everyone is secure. Do not attempt to cross over into government lines. Please listen for our instructions.

REBECCA, wearing a flak jacket and helmet enters with NILA.

REBECCA: *(Takes out her camera.)* People are carrying everything they own. *(She starts taking photos.)*

NILA: What are the UN people going to do?

REBECCA: The government are only letting us in for 24 hours. I'm going to try to gather as much information as possible while I'm here. The more information we have, the better our position will be. I'll need you to help with the interviews.

Leaflets fall from the sky. On REBECCA's walkie talkie, we hear her colleague.

RADIO: The army has created a No Fire Zone for civilians to gather and be safe from artillery attacks – running west along the A35 road from the bridge to the junction. Over.

NILA: Do you think we should go there?

REBECCA: It's very close to where the front line is. *(To colleague.)* What do you think? Over.

RADIO: Anything is better than this. We've been asking for a safe zone for a while. Over.

REBECCA: At least we'll be able to give out the supplies in one place. OK. We'll keep the army informed of our position. Over.

In the distance, we see flashes of shellfire and dull thuds – fighting going on a few kilometres away. Drones hum overhead. REBECCA stands outside a bunker and calls JENNY.

REBECCA: I just gave them our location.

JENNY: I'll call them as well. Just to make sure. What's happening above the zone?

REBECCA: The drones are passing overhead but no artillery for an hour now. We've hoisted a flag – we've got our trucks here, it's very clearly a UN site.

JENNY: How many people?

REBECCA: A sea of people. Tens of thousands at least. They've put up their tarpaulin and bits of tin leaning together. People cooking meals. We'll do the distribution tomorrow morning.

JENNY: Check in with me first thing.

REBECCA: Yeah.

She hangs up. In the background, we see a thousand tiny fires burning. Families cooking their evening meals. NILA and REBECCA lie exhausted on the ground.

NILA: Have you ever seen this many people in one place before?

REBECCA: I don't think so, no.

NILA: You see. When you are here they *(points to the sky)* are scared of you.

REBECCA: Even so.

REBECCA gets up.

NILA: Just a little bit longer.

REBECCA enters the bunker. The sun sets. We see the stars and the flashes and thuds of distant explosions.

An hour later, we hear an approaching barrage of shells and rockets crashing. NILA runs into the bunker and REBECCA emerges wearing flak jacket and helmet and tries to get a signal on the satellite phone.

REBECCA: *(Shouting on phone army command.)* We are in your No Fire Zone with a UN convoy of humanitarian supplies – tell military command to direct their fire away from this zone. I gave you the coordinates.

She positions the phone away from her to pick up the sounds of shelling/screaming.

Can you hear that? You are bombing civilians and a UN convoy. People who have just eaten their meals and gone to sleep. Redirect your fire.

(Makes another call.)

Jenny? Can you hear me? They are bombing our position/

JENNY: /Shit

REBECCA: /I don't know what to … I called them/

JENNY: /I'll deal with it. Get inside your bunker.

Something thuds on the ground in front of her.

JENNY: Rebecca? Are you … Rebecca? Are you there?

REBECCA: A young woman … it's a torso of a young woman. Some of her legs. One arm. Our vehicle is covered in … I'm going to die here aren't I? Right now, I'm waiting to die …

JENNY: Get inside your bunker.

REBECCA: Can you hear them?

Many hours later as the sun is coming up, the shelling stops. REBECCA raises the hessian flap and peers through the bunker entrance. REBECCA starts to take photos. NILA walks with her.

A MAN walks over to them. He whispers to NILA in Tamil.

NILA: *(Translating.)* That is the body of my daughter. This is some of my wife's body.

Take a photo. Take it.

REBECCA does this. NILA continues to translate and it becomes clear that some of what she is saying is her own opinion.

NILA: You see the sweet face of my child? You see it? What is your advice for me? Should I pick up my child and carry her body with me to the next place we go to? Or should I dig a grave for her here? What is the meaning of you being here? You are just pretending to help us. You're not even planning to stop it are you? People are coming up to you like you are some sort of prophet, begging you to tell everybody about this. I can't talk to the rest of the world, I can't ask anyone else. I can only ask you. Are they going to let us all die? Look at the sweet face of my child. Just 2 years old.

We see SANATH announcing.

SANATH: The last bastion of the Tamil Tigers, the town of Mullaitivu, has fallen. The battle is 95% over. Not a drop of civilian blood has been spilt by the army in this humanitarian rescue mission.

Later that day, REBECCA is leaving.

REBECCA: The Tigers will never give you a pass out of here.

NILA: I thought, by now, all of this would make sense.

REBECCA: They're recruiting anyone they can from off the streets so you need to –

NILA: Yes.

She hands NILA an envelope in a zip-lock plastic pouch.

REBECCA: A letter. In Sinhala, Tamil and English With your photo. It says you work for the UN. If they take you or … when this is over. It could help.

NILA: We are going to have nothing. After all.

VOICE ON WALKIE TALKIE: Rebecca? Over.

NILA: You need to tell them.

REBECCA: *(On walkie talkie.)* Yep. There in a minute. Over.

NILA and REBECCA embrace.

REBECCA walks past the 'checkpoint' and sleepwalks into UN headquarters in Colombo. JENNY walks towards her.

REBECCA: I had to leave them all there. Get me in a room with them.

JENNY: That won't help right now.

REBECCA: They bombed us for hours. Put me on TV. I'll tell my version.

JENNY: We need to deal with this in the right way.

REBECCA: They are controlling this story completely … no journalists are getting inside so there hasn't been one TV clip of what's going on there. I've got photos *(Produces a memory stick. JENNY takes it)*. I am a UN employee. Not a Tiger, not a Tamil. An independent witness.

JENNY: You need to think about this carefully. Five minutes on TV which the government will just brush off? Nobody here will report it – they've got the domestic press by the balls. I want to get a full briefing from you and then we'll talk to HQ about how to take this forward.

REBECCA: We need to tell people about this.

JENNY: The last 2 people from this office who challenged the government had their visas revoked. You're not going to be of use to anyone if you're out of the game.

REBECCA: How am I going to sit here every day looking at that massive billboard of the map with the red areas shrinking? Listening to those jets leaving for the north?

JENNY: You need to maintain a balance between what *is happening* and what is *possible*.

REBECCA: So tell me what is possible.

JENNY: Our mission here is not a peacekeeping one. Not a political one. We are only authorised to provide humanitarian assistance.

REBECCA: Well there are a few thousand corpses who don't really give a shit about humanitarian assistance right now. The UN counts the dead right?

JENNY: That's a big job.

REBECCA: But it's *possible*.

16.

At night. REBECCA is working at the UN office in Colombo. She's struggling to stay awake. Throughout the scene REBECCA wanders in and out of her reality, her delusions, and the world of the person she is talking to. DOCTOR appears standing behind an operating table tending to a patient with a serious war wound. His scrubs are stained with blood from non-stop surgery. He is pulling shrapnel out of the patient's leg and throwing it into a bucket that is already half full with bloody pieces of shrapnel.

REBECCA: Number of patients there now?

DOCTOR: About 400.

REBECCA: How many dead this week?

DOCTOR: Over 500 the last time I checked. Someone will send you the names.

REBECCA: Are you getting reports from the other facilities?

DOCTOR: Same story.

REBECCA: How are you managing?

DOCTOR: There are just five doctors left. We are civil servants of the government so they ordered us to leave, but we stayed without pay.

REBECCA: Supplies?

DOCTOR: Ha! This is the high-tech ICU. No cardiac monitor. No laboratory facilities. All they send is paracetamol, allergy tablets, vitamins … Not a single bottle of IV fluid, antibiotic or anaesthetic. We've had to beg for supplies from the Tigers.

The table revolves and we see another patient in pain. REBECCA watches while the DOCTOR picks up some surgical instruments and starts to make incisions in the abdominal area.

DOCTOR: Another bowel surgery. She's been ripped open.

REBECCA's phone rings. We see NICK wearing a Red Cross T-shirt making the call.

REBECCA: UNCOG.

NICK: Ah yes. In the tradition of all things UN, you need a ridiculous acronym. What is it – COG? Cog.

REBECCA: Crisis Operations Group. What have you got for me Nick?

NICK: Mayhem … in a word. Our Head of Ops broke the Red Cross code of silence last week – did you hear?

REBECCA: About bloody time too.

NICK: When are you lot going to do the same?

REBECCA: We need numbers.

NICK: This week, our Tamil staff have counted 367 dead. 657 injured. We're trying to get the injured out on the ships, but, it takes an age to get safe passage and we're getting fired at all the time.

REBECCA: Send me the documentation.

REBECCA walks over to the DOCTOR.

REBECCA: Have you eaten today? Or slept?

DOCTOR laughs and removes a blood soaked dressing from the patient and starts surgery.

DOCTOR: I've stopped giving them our coordinates. The last three times I did that, we were shelled within the day.

REBECCA: Bombing hospitals?

DOCTOR: Now I tell my staff – no cross on the roof, no GPS. Since then, we haven't been hit.

The table revolves again. The patient is always NILA from now on. She is heavily pregnant and lying on the table.

WOMAN: I need to have this baby now.

DOCTOR: When are you due?

WOMAN: Three weeks.

DOCTOR: This is not an emergency Madam.

WOMAN: In a few days we will need to run. What will happen if I'm in labour?

DOCTOR: Your first child?

WOMAN: Yes.

DOCTOR: Do you have a family member to help you?

WOMAN: My husband is missing.

REBECCA holds the hand of the patient. The DOCTOR grows an extra pair of arms, like a Hindu God. One arm makes an incision in the woman's abdomen. Another arm delivers the baby. Another arm cuts the cord and starts stitching the incision. Another arm wraps the baby in a towel and hands it to the mother. The table revolves again. This time NILA in agony, clutching at her abdomen.

DOCTOR. I'll come back to you later. (To REBECCA.) She needs antibiotics to stave off infection. She'll die.

NILA protests. Table revolves again.

DOCTOR: Ooh! Double amputation.

The DOCTOR plugs his ears with his fingers while the 2 extra arms perform the amputations. NILA screams.

REBECCA: *(To NICK.)* Numbers this week?

NICK: 690 dead. 1200 injured.

REBECCA: Jesus

ERIK: *(To REBECCA.)* We're working on a deal between the warring parties. Trying to get other nations to endorse it. I need as much information as you can give me.

REBECCA: I'm still collecting figures … I can only give you the unofficial version right now.

ERIK: Whatever you have about the situation on the ground will be useful.

REBECCA: I'll send it on.

NILA enters REBECCA's office.

NILA: Everywhere you go you see people screaming over bodies.

DOCTOR: *(To REBECCA.)* It's the adrenaline that keeps me awake.

DOCTOR hoses down the bloody operating table and sprays it with disinfectant.

NICK: Staff are reporting incidents of Tigers shooting at Tamil civilians wanting to surrender to the army.

REBECCA's mobile rings. She rushes over to get it.

REBECCA: Nila. Are you there?

NICK: The army are even shelling food distribution lines.

REBECCA: We need to verify the numbers. Triangulate the … is there anyone else who can verify what you've told me?

NICK: Apart from the doctors, there are some priests I can put you in touch with.

REBECCA: Situation in the hospitals?

NICK: Patients are lying under tables, in hallways, outside, in the driveways. Bodies everywhere.

NILA appears behind REBECCA

NILA: Why don't you get me out of here?

Everything on REBECCA's desk (lamp, folders, hole-punch, calculator, etc.) starts buzzing or ringing.

REBECCA: *(To DOCTOR.)* Did you see where the girl went – the young lady who was here? Was she hurt?

Everything buzzes/rings again.

NILA: Tell me what to do.

REBECCA: I'm trying, I'm collecting these … *(To DOCTOR.)* Have you seen her?

NILA: Get me onto a ship.

REBECCA: Early 20s. Long dark hair.

DOCTOR laughs. Phones ringing.

NILA places a watch on REBECCA' desk.

NILA: Parithi, a 50 *year old shopkeeper from Tharmapuram.*

Some more watches and personal effects (slippers, photos, important papers, gold chain) emerge from or fall onto REBECCA's desk. NILA places a number of these personal effects on front of REBECCA with each sentence.

NILA: Mrs. Kavitha. 8 months pregnant and mother of 4 year old boy. Priya is a school teacher whose husband died with her, he was a car mechanic.

NICK: Is anyone doing anything?

REBECCA: We need the figures. A credible number we can use.

NICK: Who is talking to the Tigers?

REBECCA: Why don't you answer your phone?

NILA: They are saying we need to accept the common fate of
the Tamil people.

17.

*ERIK is at his home in Oslo. As he speaks, he is ironing his shirt, getting
dressed into trousers and a shirt and eating his breakfast.*

ERIK: *(On phone to his colleague.)* I'll need a draft before I leave.
Norway, Japan, the US and the EU: Jointly express their
concern ... their *great* concern. We recognise that further
loss of life will ... will serve no cause ... No, no, don't use
the word *surrender*. That's not going to help ... cessation
... organised cessation ... or something like that. Yes, then
those 2 points about lasting peace.

*ERIK picks up an official-looking document wallet and walks out
the door into Oslo airport.*

I don't see another way. We're the only ones with access to
the Tiger leadership because we're the only ones left who
are willing to speak with them. All the big players have
proscribed them as terrorists.

The person they've arranged for us to negotiate with used
to be their arms dealer. The elusive KP has emerged from
retirement and is now the Tiger representative.

*NORWEGIAN OFFICIAL Runs up to him and puts his tie on and
gives his shoes a quick polish.*

*REBECCA puts a few pieces of paper into a manila envelope and
hands it to JENNY. They both walk into SANATH's office.*

A legendary figure. On Interpol's most wanted list. Yeah.
A big fish.

*NORWEGIAN OFFICIAL hands ERIK a suit jacket and helps him
get into it.*

18.

JENNY: The UN has a number of concerns with respect to the military operation.

SANATH: And what are your concerns?

JENNY: We urgently need to access civilians with humanitarian relief.

SANATH: Someone needs to speak to the Tigers about that. If they stopped holding their people as human shields, you would have plenty of access.

JENNY: There is a serious humanitarian crisis.

ERIK sits on a seat in a plane and fastens his seatbelt.

(Still on phone.) I'm meeting him at a hotel in the centre.

ERIK is passed an espresso. He drinks it.

Our terminology is 'an *organised end* to the war'.

ERIK removes his seatbelt and he is now in a high speed train. He removes his jacket and loosens his tie.

ANNOUNCEMENT: Journey time to the central station is 28 minutes. We are now cruising at 160km per hour.

ERIK: I'll let you know *(ends call)*.

JENNY: A pause in the fighting so we can ensure food and medical supplies get in and ensure injured people can get out.

SANATH: And give the Tigers time to regroup?

JENNY: Just a short pause. A gesture like that will be warmly welcomed internationally.

SANATH: The last time we paused, they let virtually no one out.

JENNY: The civilians have been without basic humanitarian assistance for almost a month.

SANATH: I'll raise it with my colleagues.

JENNY: We also ask for your assurances that you will no longer use heavy weapons in an area which is so densely packed with civilians.

SANATH: In all of his statements, The President has been very clear we are not doing that.

JENNY: We've been collecting numbers *(hands SANATH the envelope)*. We acknowledge the grave responsibility the Tigers bear for this situation. However, we have credibly verified that between 20 January and 5 February more than 1,000 civilians were killed and more than 2700 injured.

SANATH: What business does the UN have doing this?

REBECCA: The UN is the only independent body capable of making an educated guess on casualty figures, based on the network of sources that we have.

JENNY: It's standard practice.

SANATH: What is your methodology?

REBECCA: When one party of people report deaths in a certain location, we cross-check those reports … then come up with a *conservative* estimate of the number of people killed.

SANATH: So, this here is … word of mouth?

JENNY: It's the only possible way to do it.

SANATH: I've told you many times that this war is an internal matter. *(To JENNY.)* We were very clear with you about that when we approved your posting here.

REBECCA: When you bomb civilians and UN positions, it is no longer an internal matter.

SANATH: How are you able to ascertain that these dead people are not Tamil Tiger fighters?

REBECCA: A large number of the dead are women, children and the elderly.

SANATH: Just because a person is wearing a sarong or a sari and has been injured, up there, that does not prove that person is a civilian. They have all received weapons training. They are all sympathisers. Little boys have blown up our soldiers with grenades.

JENNY: Our sources are reliable.

REBECCA: Government doctors – your own civil servants – holding the hospitals together. Jesuit priests. We spoke with the Red Cross who are now expressing public concern about this.

SANATH: We have a zero civilian casualty policy. The civilians who are dying are dying because of Tiger fire. Your sources are in the zone and have a biased view and are most likely doing the Tigers' bidding.

SANATH hands the envelope to JENNY. She takes it.

I would like you to go back and review your methodology, in particular, how you are ensuring the dead you are counting are not Tiger fighters – then please come back to me.

JENNY and SANATH shake hands.

REBECCA and JENNY exit.

ANNOUNCEMENT: We hope you enjoy your stay in Kuala Lumpur.

ERIK walks into a hotel room where he shakes hands with KP, a softly spoken man in business attire. They stand in front of a big window overlooking the Kuala Lumpur city skyline. A neon lamp of the border of Tamil Eelam is on a nearby table.

REBECCA: *(Points to the envelope.)* This is the only leverage we've got. We can't just give them a free hand.

JENNY: I need to ensure we have access to the camps for those who are getting out … we need to maintain our grip on the humanitarian operation.

REBECCA: We haven't had humanitarian access for a month. What makes you think we'll get it later? You heard him – we can spend the next month examining our methodology – they will just keep disputing it.

JENNY: The UN is always more relevant when these things are finished.

REBECCA: These 'things'? At least go public with these figures.

JENNY: I've been saying thousands of casualties to the media and in my statements.

REBECCA: But not attributing the vast majority to the government.

JENNY: We're not the bad guys.

REBECCA: Tell me how making this public is not going to save lives?

JENNY: Because I think the government will react by expelling the UN from the country, closing the camps to the outside world, shutting off all external assistance and then bombing the Tamils without a shred of restraint. The more pressure that is brought to bear – the more quickly they feel they need to get this done, which means more carnage.

REBECCA: Or they might stop using heavy weapons, fortify their positions and move in slowly. Whatever happens, happens. But shouldn't we be telling the world what we know? What we categorically know?

19.

KP: I was one of those young men who joined the struggle in the 70s. Many of us joined. Those memories are still very strong. Bala was fond of you.

ERIK: And now the negotiating falls to you.

KP: I'm just as surprised as you. But when your leader asks you, of course you can't refuse. You've met the leader, no?

ERIK: I was permitted to meet Prabhakaran a total of ten times. More times than any other non-Tamil. He was surprising. Short. Soft hands. You expect hardness and an expression of ... weariness or ... You expect to be spoken to in a certain way. But I remember thinking he was shy. We used to eat lunch together. We talked about cooking and history and the films he liked. Anything with Clint Eastwood in it. It was the closest any non-Tamil could get.

KP: He wants a ceasefire.

ERIK: No chance.

KP: And the UN?

ERIK: The Rajapakse government has played the game well. It was quite brilliantly done actually. The Chinese are on their side, India has been hands-off for years but are giving vital intelligence to the government.

REBECCA and JENNY enter SANATH's office. REBECCA hands the SANATH a manila envelope with some papers inside.

REBECCA: 7,721 confirmed dead. 18,479 confirmed injured. Mostly the result of government shelling. These are counted bodies. Thousands have simply been buried in their bunkers. It's a gross underestimate.

ERIK: *(Points to the envelope.)* There is a way forward. An organised end to this. The US, India, Japan, the EU, and senior figures in the UN in New York have all backed this deal. *(Handing envelope to KP. He doesn't take it.)* The result of many weeks of secret negotiations.

SANATH: Have you altered your methodology as we discussed?

REBECCA: I was there. I saw it and I smelled it. The Tigers do not have Israeli jets. You've got radar targeting equipment, drones, army infiltrators have easy access to the population. You know when you're firing into densely packed areas. You know you're killing civilians. You're committing every war crime in the book.

SANATH: Look at that. You're practically foaming at the mouth. A very passionate young colleague you have here. Now correct me if I'm wrong, but you're a relatively junior member of staff?

REBECCA: I lived there for four years. I saw 100% more than what you have seen of that place.

SANATH: Oh, I see. Another White Tigress. Jenny, you really should monitor for this sort of bias in your office.

REBECCA: I know what I saw.

SANATH: I admire strong feelings like yours. I really do. I wonder, do you start foaming at the mouth whenever your government does the same thing? You dare to come in here and wag your finger at us.

ERIK: *(To KP.)* As a guerrilla outfit, you're behind the times. Nobody wants anything to do with suicide bombers and child soldiers. You lost your just cause.

KP: You must be careful to judge. People have starved themselves to the death, have taken cyanide, have been blown apart and decapitated for this cause.

SANATH: You have not grown up with war and lived with the hope that you and your children won't die with war.

KP: When did you see your first mutilated corpse lying on the road?

SANATH: You grew up expecting a future.

KP: We grew up expecting a fight for our future.

SANATH: You are so concerned with *numbers*. Do you know the number of dead Iraqis as a result of the war waged by your governments?

REBECCA: We are not here to discuss the crimes of others.

SANATH: 120,000 civilian casualties and counting. And that is not including the number who died as a result of sanctions imposed on Iraq by your colleagues, the great and the good at the UN Security Council for 13 years prior to the invasion. Any idea about that *number*? At least half a million *children* dead.

JENNY: We represent the *international* community's concern about civilians being killed in huge numbers.

SANATH: Our soldiers are giving their lives to make sure Prabhakaran and his men are stopped. Over 5,000 mother's sons in the last few years have been erased from this world in the name of that objective. When we defeat the Tigers, there will be peace in this country. All your nations have achieved in the name of fighting terrorism is perpetual war.

What you don't see is that your nations and your colleagues in New York want us to get this done. It is a headache for them. And we are doing it in the way we think is best.

(To REBECCA.) Your government *(to REBECCA)* has been selling us arms for years. Yours *(to JENNY)* has been supplying vital intelligence to us to support the military operation. We're about to be given a $2.5 billion loan from the IMF. China, Pakistan and Israel are re-arming us.

KP: He asked me to negotiate a ceasefire. That is all he is prepared to do.

ERIK: Impossible.

KP: 50,000 people demonstrating on the streets of London. 45,000 in Toronto and that number will grow.

ERIK: All Tamil. Waving Tamil Tiger flags! No pink faces in the crowds.

KP: The UN must be monitoring the situation. They acted on Gaza last month.

ERIK: When it comes to international action, 10 Palestinians killed by Israelis goes for 1000 in Sri Lanka and maybe

10,000 in the Congo. Sri Lanka is not in that league of nations that invites military intervention. Too distant. Too small. Too insignificant and too much in the Indian and Chinese spheres of influence. It will never reach the top of the pile.

KP sits down and reads the paperwork.

SANATH: We want his head. Just like you wanted Saddam's. Just like you want Bin Laden's. Crushing him while he is down. That is something no government would be able to resist. That man has escaped our clutches so many times and we are not prepared to put a stop to this operation until we have his head. I want my nation to be prosperous and peaceful. You don't care about that. You'll be on a flight to the next country soon.

Whenever I have a conversation with investors, economists, it always ends with the word 'but'. They all say yes you have all these extraordinary features, *but*, you have a war going on. And now, for the first time, we can see that we're going to win. And winners are not prosecuted for war crimes.

REBECCA: Your victory will have no legitimacy. It will be a PR disaster for you and it will play directly into the hands of the Tigers.

SANATH: There will be no Tigers when we're finished. We do it now or it takes another 10 years, 20 years to do it. Thousands will die in any case.

A microphone is placed in front of JENNY. She is answering questions from the diplomatic corps in Colombo. REBECCA watches.

AMBASSADOR 1: *(British.)* When are you likely to publish the figures?

JENNY: Publication of figures on the mounting civilian casualties could incite adverse reactions from extremist elements in Sri Lankan society and jeopardise our mission here.

AMBASSADOR 2: *(German.)* Our government is willing to exert diplomatic pressure– but we need your confirmation on the figures.

JENNY: Messages will be conveyed through appropriate channels without going overboard.

AMBASSADOR 3: *(American.)* Can you give us at least a ballpark?

JENNY: The civilian casualties have certainly been, and continue to be, heavy, but the detailed figures are still hard to be sure about.

REBECCA and JENNY in JENNY's office.

JENNY: I'm not going head to head with this government and no one above me is telling me otherwise.

REBECCA: I just spent 2 months doing this. Something that I thought would be used, at least in some small way. And it's going to end up in some classified UN black hole somewhere, isn't it?

JENNY: In this case, a judgement has been made at HQ that it is better to be here and be silent than not be here at all. I know when I'm beaten.

REBECCA: They were perfectly happy to put out 1000 killed in Gaza a couple of months back and those figures were based on a much less precise methodology. We're the United fucking Nations. Here to protect. They are one, small, developing country. If not us, then who?

JENNY: I've been in many rooms with many men like him. And I don't listen to what they say anymore. I try and figure out what is at the bottom of their gut. Ringing the alarm bells a bit louder will make it uncomfortable for them, but nothing is going to stop them going for the kill.

REBECCA: Is this what they call the international community then?

REBECCA addressed by a member of the diplomatic corps.

AMBASSADOR: *(American.)* I know plenty of international news desks that will report this.

REBECCA. But they need a source.

ERIK: We and other nations have made many diplomatic attempts to stop the Sri Lankan government from bombing. Nothing has worked. However, they have agreed, reluctantly, if Prabhakaran accepts, to an amnesty for all rebel fighters who will surrender, along with all the civilians, to the UN or the Red Cross, and they will register each person.

KP: *(Reading.)* ' … with the exception of Mr Prabhakaran and his intelligence chief who would be put in internationally supervised custody'.

ERIK: I have offered to go to the war zone. So has Ban Ki-moon. To ensure it's done properly. An internationally mediated laying down of arms. An American naval ship will take civilians.

KP: Prabhakaran will be evacuated before the army get close.

ERIK: You have barely any territory left. What you have is on the coast. On an island. It is surrounded. Cut off from supplies. Finished.

KP: He will be thinking many things right now. He will be weighing up different strategies every hour of every day. But if I know one thing about the leader, the one thing that comes before everything else is a separate state of Tamil Eelam. It is well known that Prabhakaran told his bodyguard to shoot him the moment he gave that up. He wants to see it in his lifetime.

ERIK: Tell him Arafat didn't see it in his lifetime. Tell him that intensifying the distress of his people will not increase the pressure for international action.

The world doesn't care. The world does not care. The world doesn't even *know* this is happening. There are European tourists sipping cocktails at this moment on the beaches in Colombo, who have no idea.

The only reason I'm here is because I know what they don't – that hundreds of thousands of people are being shelled constantly, starved, dying of their injuries, hiding in hand-dug trenches while we stand here looking at the skyline. This *(refers to the surrender deal)* will at least limit the horror. It is a good deal. There will be no better deal than this.

SANATH stands and makes a public announcement on TV.

SANATH: Civilian casualty figures were recently compiled by the UN and leaked to the media. However, I have been in communication with the UN's office in Colombo and they have clarified the situation:

JENNY: *(Speaks into a microphone.)* Circumstances did not permit us to independently verify casualty estimates on the ground.

SANATH: Therefore …

JENNY: We do not have verifiable figures of how many casualties there were.

SANATH: The assertion that two-thirds of casualties had occurred in the No Fire Zone were described as –

JENNY: Unsubstantiated.

REBECCA hands JENNY an envelope.

REBECCA: My resignation.

KP: *(To ERIK.)* Prabhakaran has considered the offer. He has just three words. This is unacceptable.

ERIK: This is how he wants to be remembered?

KP: He believes that nations are built on blood. You know your own history well enough. Your people have resisted oppressive forces, been an oppressive force, they have been ravaged and poor and they have fought to be taken seriously as an independent nation. Your modern, peace-loving social democracy is built on centuries of bloodshed.

20.

NILA is lying alone in a trench dug in the sand. The photo of her mother sits illuminated in front of her. Bullets, blasts and jets scream above her. Slowly, a woman emerges from the sand and embraces NILA from behind. Her face and arms are caked with mud and sand.

WOMAN: This is not the end. Did you hear me?

NILA nods.

WOMAN: You're not like the others up there. They are not like you. What you need to do when you see the dead is to draw a line between them and you. They shall not infect you. You are nothing to them in the sky and you are nothing the ones holding on with their last breath to this pathetic strip of beach. You are meat to them. But to me. To me. You need to remember this: I am your mother and you are my daughter. You are my wonderful girl. How could you die? I can feel your heart beating. I can see the future and I can see you walking along in it.

Those jets – it's just silly men who are flying them. And silly men who are firing. You should laugh at them. Will you laugh at them? *(WOMAN grabs at NILA's face from behind.)* Will you?

You need to get across the lagoon and go to the army's side. You take what you need. You walk on the dead. You suck the blood from them. Crush their bones and their hearts and their lungs beneath your feet. Polar bear cubs are born deaf and blind beneath the snow, but eventually they grow into the one of the largest, most powerful animals on this earth. This is in your blood. You were born in war and you know how to look it in the eye.

NILA frees herself from the embrace and the WOMAN goes limp. NILA takes the WOMAN's hands in her hands and kisses them all over and then her face, the way a grieving relative would kiss a corpse in an open coffin.

NILA starts crawling across the beach. Bullets whizz past. As she crawls different pairs of hands clutch at her ankles. At the same time, ERIK is in Oslo watching television. REBECCA is receiving Facebook messages: 'I survived. I'm in Cape Town' ... Priya and her sister have died.' ... 'Three more from the office were killed.' ... 'Zurich, Sydney'.

ERIK, REBECCA and SANATH receive a text message announcing Prabhakaran's death.

ANNOUNCEMENT: The leader of the Tamil Tigers, Vellupilai Prabhakaran, has been shot dead with 2 of his senior leaders while trying to escape the war zone, marking the end of Asia's longest running civil war.

Images of Prabhakaran's corpse. NILA wades through grey waters of the lagoon, walking on the dead, body parts floating around her.

ANNOUNCEMENT: In many towns and cities there was dancing and singing in the streets, with crowds waving Sri Lanka's flag.

21.

SANATH appears before a lectern. A bouquet of flowers is attached to the front of the podium. A screen behind the official reads: 'Defeating Terrorism: The Sri Lankan Experience. Galadari Hotel, Colombo. 31 May- 2 June 2011'.

NILA is pushed out of a van and her handcuffs are removed. She takes off her blindfold.

Applause.

SANATH: It is a pleasure and a privilege for me to address you at this seminar organized by the Sri Lanka Army: 'Defeating Terrorism-The Sri Lankan Experience'. *(Points to the screen and smiles.)*

> *NILA is quickly given a bag, a coat and a passport.*

On behalf of the Government of Sri Lanka, I am particularly proud to welcome our distinguished foreign delegates from 41 nations.

> *NILA sits at an airport waiting to board a flight.*

ANNOUNCEMENT: The makeshift camps where civilians are being held are being financed by the United Nations, but no international observers have been allowed access.

SANATH: This seminar takes place at an opportune moment, just 2 years after the world's greatest humanitarian rescue operation and this country's victory over the brutal terrorism of Tamil Tigers. None of you gentlemen believed that Sri Lanka would be at this stage today.

> *REBECCA receives another Facebook message: 'Hello Rebecca. Are you OK?' She types back 'Nila? Where are you?' Response – 'Croydon'.*

SANATH: A number of influential figures in the international community formed very strong opinions, or should I say, jumped to very hasty conclusions about our conduct of the war.

REBECCA is sitting with NILA in London. NILA is wearing a drab tracksuit. She invites REBECCA to look at the wounds on her body.

ANNOUNCEMENT: A UN panel has found reports of up to 40,000 dead credible, most of them killed in the final onslaught, and there are signs that the final death toll could be a lot higher.

REBECCA and NILA sit in a TV studio. They have lapel mics fixed.

VOICE OF TECHNICIAN: Just checking the levels. Mic 1 – what did you have for breakfast?

NILA: No breakfast.

VOICE OF TECHNICIAN: Mic 2.

REBECCA: Um, toast, I think.

VOICE OF TECHNICIAN: I'm gonna need you to chat for a bit.

REBECCA: Right. OK *(To NILA.)* so I can start by saying that when people here think about Sri Lanka they think lovely beaches, good honeymoon destination, cricket.

VOICE OF TECHNICIAN: Good, good. Mic1.

NILA: It will take time for people to know about what happened. But they will. A day will come. They will be remembered. The dead have power that nobody can control.

SANATH: I hope that, while you are here, you will see something of our country, its scenic beauty, the formal hospitality of its people, the vibrancy of our cultural traditions and that you will take back home with you happy memories of this island and its contribution to the peace and the stability of the world.

ERIK turns off the TV.

WWW.OBERONBOOKS.COM

Follow us on www.twitter.com/@oberonbooks
& www.facebook.com/OberonBooksLondon

Printed in the USA
CPSIA information can be obtained
at www.ICGtesting.com
LVHW020942171024
794056LV00003B/923